Build an Aquarium

by Stephanie Hayes

PEARSON
Scott Foresman

DK

What You Already Know

An ecosystem is all the living and nonliving things in an area. The nonliving parts of an ecosystem include air, water, soil, temperature, and sunlight. An ecosystem's living parts are made up of populations, or groups of organisms of one species that live in an area at the same time. All of the populations in the ecosystem together are called a community. Each organism has a niche, or job within the ecosystem. Organisms also have habitats, or homes.

Scientists have divided the world into biomes, or large ecosystems. You may know of tropical rainforests, grasslands, and deserts. Other biomes include taigas, deciduous forests, and tundras. Water biomes include rivers, wetlands, coral reefs, and the deep sea.

The ocean is a huge ecosystem that contains several biomes.

All living things need energy. Energy moves through ecosystems in food chains. Organisms at the beginning of the chain produce energy, which is then consumed by organisms further along the chain. When energy passes from one organism to another, a little bit has always been lost. There is less total energy at the top of the chain than at the bottom. This is called the energy pyramid, since the amount of energy gets smaller as you go up, like a pyramid.

In ecosystems, substances are passed from one organism to another again and again. Nitrogen, carbon dioxide, and oxygen cycle through every ecosystem.

In every ecosystem, living and nonliving things are constantly interacting. Aquariums are very small ecosystems created by humans. In this book, you will learn how the animals in an aquarium interact with each other and their environment.

An aquarium is a very small ecosystem.

Getting Started

When setting up an aquarium's ecosystem, it is very important to make it as close to your fish's natural habitat as you can. In the wild, the organisms in a fish's home would keep its ecosystem in balance. In an aquarium, you will have to do this job. The tank should also be set up with plants, rocks, and other objects that your fish would find in the wild. If you want more than one kind of fish in your aquarium, you should choose types that will live peacefully with each other. It is a good idea to have each fish fill a different niche in the community.

It is important to understand what a fish is before planning an aquarium. Fish are cold-blooded vertebrates that live in all kinds of water habitats. You should set up your aquarium to be like the habitat your specific fish has in the wild. Fish use fins to move through the water. Instead of breathing air through lungs as many land animals do, fish use gills to get oxygen from the water. There are three kinds of fish—jawless, cartilaginous, and bony. Read on to learn more about these three types of fish.

Tropical blue, yellow, and green ram cichlids are good community fish.

Kinds of Fish

The lamprey is a jawless fish. It has smooth skin without scales, and looks like an eel. Growing to thirty-six inches in length, the lamprey has a round mouth lined with small teeth. It uses this mouth to attach itself to other fish. The lamprey lives by sucking the blood of other fish. This sometimes causes the other fish to die.

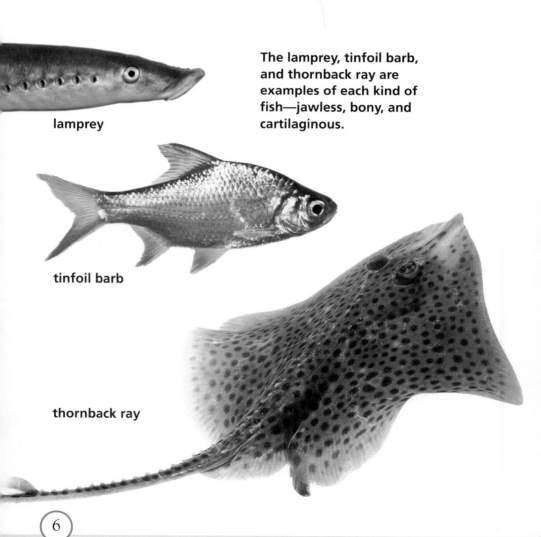

lamprey

The lamprey, tinfoil barb, and thornback ray are examples of each kind of fish—jawless, bony, and cartilaginous.

tinfoil barb

thornback ray

Sharks and rays are cartilaginous fish, which means that their skeletons are made of cartilage instead of bone. Cartilage is a strong, flexible, rubberlike material. Thornback rays can grow to three feet in length. They have rough skin with thorny spikes on their winglike fins, backs, and long, thin tails. Thornback rays eat fish, shrimp, and other crustaceans, grinding them with rows of flat teeth.

Bony fish have skeletons made of bone. They also have platelike scales, gills, and a swim bladder—an organ full of air that helps them float. The tinfoil barb is a fast swimmer with a deep tail fin and thin body. These tropical fish eat both plants and animals and grow to thirteen inches in length. They swim in schools of five or more.

A school of parrotfish swim in shallow water.

Aquarium Ecosystems

In the wild all the parts of an ecosystem work together to keep the ecosystem healthy. Falling rain cleans the water and adds oxygen. The Sun's energy helps plants and algae grow. When animals eat the plants and algae, the energy is passed on to them. Animals take in oxygen and breathe out carbon dioxide. Plants absorb carbon dioxide, which they use to make food, and release oxygen back into the air. Bacteria help stop dangerous levels of chemicals from building up in the water.

Falling rain and sunlight help keep natural ecosystems healthy.

In an aquarium most of these details must be balanced by the person setting up the tank. By carefully choosing the fish, plants, rocks, and filter used in the aquarium, we can copy the fish's natural ecosystem and keep it healthy. Different ecosystems must be created for different kinds of fish.

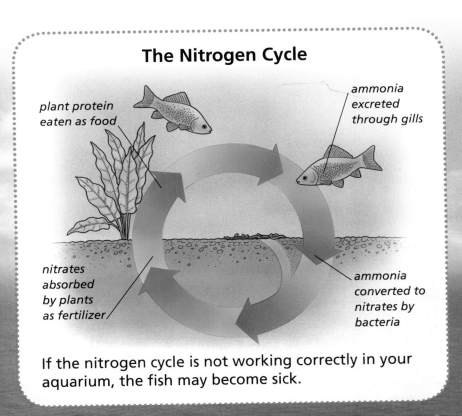

The Nitrogen Cycle

plant protein eaten as food

ammonia excreted through gills

nitrates absorbed by plants as fertilizer

ammonia converted to nitrates by bacteria

If the nitrogen cycle is not working correctly in your aquarium, the fish may become sick.

Tank Equipment

One of the first things to choose when setting up an aquarium is the material to cover the bottom of the tank. This material can filter the water, make the tank look nice, and give plants a place to grow. Plants make oxygen for the fish to breathe and make the tank seem more like a natural habitat. Plants need light, so you'll need an electric light for the tank. If you choose ocean fish, you'll have to add just the right amount of salt to your tank. A special tool called a hydrometer should be used to check salt levels.

Natural materials make the tank more like the fish's wild habitat.

rock   slate

Tanks should be chosen keeping in mind the size and number of fish you would like to have.

gravel   bogwood

You should check your tank's pH, ammonia, and nitrate levels.

thermometer

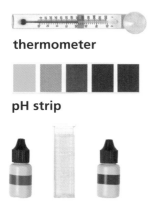

pH strip

water quality test kit

scouring pads   scrubbing brush   sponge

net   bucket   sieve

These tools are used to clean the tank and change its water.

Filtering the tank's water is very important. Mechanical filters remove gravel and extra food, chemical filters remove pollutants, and biological filters take care of fish waste. Filters also churn the water, which adds oxygen to the tank. Good oxygen levels, filtering, and a clean tank are needed for safe pH levels. pH is the amount of acid or base in the water. Some fish prefer water with more acid, some with less.

The filter adds oxygen and removes waste.

Cold-Water Tank

Cold-water tanks can house half as many fish as tropical tanks. Cold-water fish need the temperature to stay low, because cold water holds more oxygen than warm water. If the water gets too warm, the fish won't get enough oxygen, and they will become sick. Goldfish are cold-water fish. There are many kinds of goldfish, including shubunkins, the common goldfish, comets, sarasa comets, and calico fantails.

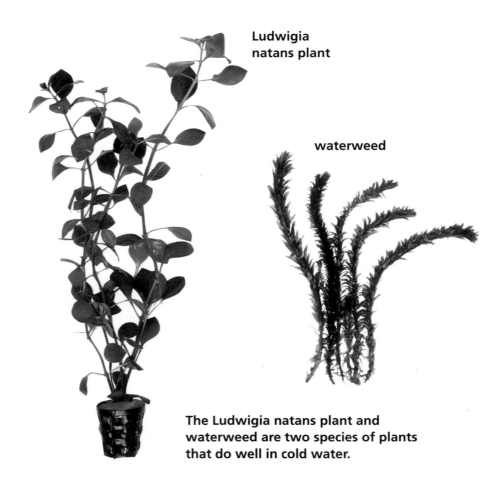

Ludwigia natans plant

waterweed

The Ludwigia natans plant and waterweed are two species of plants that do well in cold water.

Goldfish and other cold-water fish live at lower temperatures than tropical fish.

shubunkin

common goldfish

sarasa comet

comet

calico fantail

Plants for cold-water aquariums live best at temperatures of 50°F–77°F. Water pennywort has a tall stem with heart-shaped leaves and small roots. Java fern has eight-inch leaves and roots to rocks very well. The anacharis can be free floating or rooted. It is good goldfish food and adds a lot of oxygen to the tank.

Fish can be added to a tank by carefully using a net.

Goldfish like a water temperature of 52°F–72°F. They can grow to twenty-two inches long but will stay small if they live in a small tank. Goldfish usually swim in the middle of the tank but will come to the surface to eat. They will eat as much food as they are given, so be careful not to feed them too much. Goldfish do not have eyelids and are sensitive to light, so tank lights should not be suddenly turned on in a dark room. Turn the room light on first!

A home aquarium is a good way to observe a community of fish.

The weather loach is another cold-water fish. It can grow to be twelve inches long and does well in a temperature of no more than 72°F. Loaches have long, thin bodies like eels. They live at the bottom of the tank, where they eat food that other fish have missed. They also dig up and eat plants. When the air pressure gets lower because of a storm, the weather loach becomes more active. This is where it gets its name. Loaches' tanks should have a strong top, called a hood, or else they may jump out. They like to hide, so the tank should have rocks or other objects in it.

Tropical Tanks

It is important to have a heater in a tropical tank for the same reason it is important to keep a cold-water tank cool. The wrong temperature means the water will have the wrong amount of oxygen in it, and the fish will get sick. A thermometer should be used to check that the heater is working well. There are two kinds of heaters. One is a tube with heating coils inside, hung inside the tank. The other kind is placed on the bottom of the tank. This allows the heat to rise through the water. Tropical tanks should be kept between 72°F and 80°F.

twisted eelgrass

water wisteria

dwarf cryptocoryne

broad-leaf Amazon sword

All of these plants grow well in tropical aquariums.

bronze corydoras

sunset platy

female guppy

zebra danio

male guppy

rosy barb

Guppies, danios, barbs, and catfish can all
be kept in tropical fish tanks.

One plant that does well in a tropical tank is the broad-leaf Amazon sword. This plant has long, green leaves and is easy to care for. The dwarf anubias and dwarf cryptocoryne are also good for the warmer waters of tropical tanks.

There are many different kinds of fish that need tropical aquariums. The blue damselfish has a long, blue body with black head markings. It is best kept in a tank alone or in a small group because it may bite other fish. Blue damselfish are omnivores, eating both plants and small animals. Their tanks should contain coral and other hiding places.

Sunset platys are strong freshwater tropical fish that grow to two and a half inches. Feeding them different foods can make their colors brighter and also keeps them in good health.

Guppies come in many colors and can grow to two inches long. They are omnivorous, and should be kept at temperatures between 62°F and 75°F.

The rosy barb can grow to six inches. The males have a rosy red belly.

rosy barb

Zebra danios have dark blue and silver stripes. They are peaceful omnivores that grow to two inches. They swim in schools at all levels of their tanks.

Panda corydoras are catfish that live at the bottom of an aquarium. They grow to be one and a half inches long and have light colored bodies with large, dark spots on their head, back, and tail fins. They like temperatures of 72°F–77°F.

Tropical fish are much more colorful than those found in cold-water tanks.

zebra danio

Themed Tanks

Some very good aquarium keepers like to set up themed tanks. These are aquariums that are very close copies of specific natural ecosystems. When copying an ecosystem, you should understand that choosing fish isn't the only thing to think about. You must think about the pH, water movement, and the kind of materials at the bottom of the tank. Plants, temperature, and exposure to light are also very important concerns.

The Papua New Guinea Sandy River tank should be thick with plants in order to match the river ecosystem.

Goldie River rainbowfish

Plants in the Zaire River tank need to be well anchored to withstand the current.

The Zaire River rapids tank is a themed tank with two areas. One of them should have lots of churning water with large pebbles for ground cover. The other part of the tank should have calmer waters and smaller pebbles. The water should be high in oxygen and very clean, with temperatures of 76°F–79°F. Plants should include *Anubias* and African water ferns. African glass catfish and red-eyed tetras are good fish for this tank.

Starting your own aquarium is not the only way to see beautiful fish up close. Public aquariums give people the chance to see animals from all over the world. At the public aquarium, you can see fish that you could never get a look at in the wild. There are rare fish and fish from very deep in the ocean. Public aquariums can also have animals that would be too large or difficult to take care of in a home aquarium.

Aquariums aren't just for fun, either. Scientists use them to study fish and other underwater life. This can help people to better understand and protect these amazing animals. Setting up an aquarium is a great way to learn about nature. It can teach you how all the parts of an ecosystem work together and let you watch fish do all the things they do in the wild.

At the aquarium you can see strange and beautiful fish from all over the world.

Glossary

algae   plantlike organisms that live in water

aquarium   a water-filled habitat made by humans for fish, plants, or other underwater life

bacteria   microorganisms that may be harmful or helpful to their environments

omnivore   an animal which feeds on both plants and other animals

pH   amount of acid or base in water. pH is given as a number, with 7.0 being equal acid and base. A higher number means more base, and a lower number means more acid.

tropical   hot and humid

vertebrate   an animal with a backbone